BENEDICT XVI

THE FATHERS & WRITERS OF THE FIRST MILLENNIUM

The Spiritual Masters

CATHOLIC TRUTH SOCIETY
PUBLISHERS TO THE HOLY SEE

Cover credit: *Rabanus Maurus offering his book to Pope Gregory I*, miniature, Ms. 340/1, f. 39v, Bibliothèque Municipale, Douai, France
Picture credit on pages 6-7: *Baptism of the Teutons and martyrdom of St Boniface*, miniature, 2° Cod.Ms.Theol. 231 Cim., f. 87r, Universitätsbibliothek, Göttingen 6-7

Original Italian edition: *Benedetto XVI: I Maestri, Padri e Scrittori del primo millennio*
© 2009 by Libreria Editrice Vaticana, Vatican City. All rights reserved

This translated edition published in the UK 2011 by the Incorporated Catholic Truth Society, London

Printed and bound by LEGO Spa, Italy

ISBN 978-1-86082-722-8

CONTENTS

John Climacus

Iwould like to return to presenting the great writers of the Church of the East and of the West in the Middle Ages. And I am proposing the figure of John known as Climacus, a Latin transliteration of the Greek term *klimakos*, which means *of the ladder* (*klimax*). This is the title of his most important work in which he describes the ladder of human life ascending towards God. He was born in about 575 a.d. He lived, therefore, during the years in which Byzantium, the capital of the Roman Empire of the East, experienced the greatest crisis in its history. The geographical situation of the Empire suddenly changed and the torrent of barbarian invasions swept away all its structures. Only the structure of the Church withstood them, continuing in these difficult times to carry out her missionary, human, social and cultural action, especially through the network of monasteries in which great religious figures such as John Climacus were active.

John Climacus with St George and St Blaise, detail, Russian Museum, St Petersburg

John lived and told of his spiritual experiences in the Mountains of Sinai, where Moses encountered God and Elijah heard his voice. Information on him has been preserved in a brief *Life* (*PG* 88, 596-608), written by a monk, Daniel of Raithu. At the age of 16, John, who had become a monk on Mount Sinai, made himself a disciple of Abba Martyr, an "elder", that is, a "wise man". At about 20 years of age, he chose to live as a hermit in a grotto at the foot of the mountain in the locality of Tola, eight kilometres from the present-day St Catherine's Monastery. Solitude, however, did not prevent him from meeting people eager for spiritual direction, or from paying visits to several monasteries near Alexandria. In fact, far from being an escape from the world and human reality, his eremitical retreat led to ardent love for others (*Life*, 5) and for God (*ibid.,* 7). After 40 years of life as a hermit, lived in love for God and for neighbour, years in which he wept, prayed and fought with demons, he was appointed hegumen of the large monastery on Mount Sinai and thus returned to cenobitic life in a monastery. However, several years before his death, nostalgic for the eremitical life, he handed over the government of the community to his brother, a monk in the same monastery.

John died after the year 650. He lived his life between two mountains, Sinai and Tabor and one can truly say that he radiated the light which Moses saw on Sinai and which was contemplated by the three Apostles on Mount Tabor!

He became famous, as I have already said, through his work, entitled *The Climax*, in the West known as the *Ladder of Divine Ascent* (*PG* 88, 632-1164). Composed at the insistent request of the hegumen of the neighbouring Monastery of Raithu in Sinai, the *Ladder* is a complete treatise of spiritual life in which John describes the monk's journey from renunciation of the world to the perfection of love. This journey according to his book covers 30 steps, each one of which is linked to the next. The journey may be summarised in three consecutive stages: the first is expressed in renunciation of the world in order to return to a state of evangelical childhood. Thus, the essential is not the renunciation but rather the connection with what Jesus said, that is, the return to true childhood in the spiritual sense, becoming like children. John comments: "A good foundation of three layers and three pillars is: innocence, fasting and temperance. Let all babes in Christ (cf. 1 *Cor* 3: 1) begin with these virtues, taking as their model the natural babes" (1, 20; 636). Voluntary detachment from beloved people and places permits the soul to enter into deeper communion with God. This renunciation leads to obedience which is the way to humility through humiliations which will never be absent on the part of the brethren. John comments: "Blessed is he who has mortified his will to the very end and has entrusted the care of himself to his teacher in the Lord: indeed he will be placed on the right hand of the Crucified One!" (4, 37; 704).

The second stage of the journey consists in spiritual combat against the passions. Every step of the ladder is linked to a principal passion that is defined and diagnosed, with an indication of the treatment and a proposal of the corresponding virtue. All together, these steps of the ladder undoubtedly constitute the most important treatise of spiritual strategy that we possess. The struggle against the passions, however, is steeped in the positive – it does not remain as something negative – thanks to the image of the "fire" of the Holy Spirit: that "all those who enter upon the good fight (cf. 1 *Tm* 6: 12), which is hard and narrow... may realise that they must leap into the fire, if they really expect the celestial fire to dwell in them" (1,18; 636). The fire of the Holy Spirit is the fire of love and truth. The power of the Holy Spirit alone guarantees victory.

However, according to John Climacus it is important to be aware that the passions are not evil in themselves; they become so through human freedom's wrong use of them. If they are purified, the passions reveal to man the path towards God with energy unified by ascesis and grace and, "if they have received from the Creator an order and a beginning..., the limit of virtue is boundless" (26/2, 37; 1068).

The last stage of the journey is Christian perfection that is developed in the last seven steps of the *Ladder*. These are the highest stages of spiritual life, which can be experienced by the "Hesychasts": the solitaries, those who have attained quiet and inner peace; but these stages are also accessible to the more fervent cenobites. Of the first three simplicity, humility and discernment John, in line with the Desert Fathers, considered the ability to discern, the most important. Every type of behaviour must be subject to discernment; everything, in fact, depends on one's deepest motivations, which need to be closely examined. Here one enters into the soul of the person and it is a question of reawakening in the hermit, in the Christian, spiritual sensitivity and a "feeling heart", which are gifts from God: "After God, we ought to follow our conscience as a rule and guide in everything," (26/1,5; 1013). In this way one reaches tranquillity of soul, *hesychia*, by means of which the soul may gase upon the abyss of the divine mysteries.

The state of quiet, of inner peace, prepares the Hesychast for prayer which in John is twofold: "corporeal prayer" and "prayer of the heart". The former is proper to those who need the help of bodily movement: stretching out the hands, uttering groans, beating the breast, etc. (15, 26; 900). The latter is spontaneous, because it is an effect of the reawakening of spiritual sensitivity,

Vision of John Climacus, Russian Museum, St Petersburg

a gift of God to those who devote themselves to corporeal prayer. In John this takes the name "Jesus prayer" (*Iesou euche*), and is constituted in the invocation of solely Jesus' name, an invocation that is continuous like breathing: "May your remembrance of Jesus become one with your breathing, and you will then know the usefulness of *hesychia*", inner peace (27/2, 26; 1112). At the end the prayer becomes very simple: the word "Jesus" simply becomes one with the breath.

The last step of the ladder (30), suffused with "the sober inebriation of the spirit", is dedicated to the supreme "trinity of virtues": faith, hope and above all charity. John also speaks of charity as *eros* (human love), a symbol of the matrimonial union of the soul with God, and once again chooses the image of fire to express the fervour, light and purification of love for God. The power of human love can be reoriented to God, just as a cultivated olive may be grafted on to a wild olive tree (cf. *Rm* 11: 24) (cf. 15, 66; 893). John is convinced that an intense experience of this *eros* will help the soul to advance far more than the harsh struggle against the passions, because of its great power. Thus, in our journey, the positive aspect prevails. Yet charity is also seen in close relation to hope: "Hope is the power that drives love. Thanks to hope, we can look forward to the reward of charity... Hope is the doorway of love... The absence of hope destroys charity: our efforts are bound to it, our labours are sustained by it, and through it we are enveloped by the mercy of God" (30, 16; 1157). The conclusion of the *Ladder* contains the synthesis of the work in words that the author has God himself utter: "May this ladder teach you the spiritual disposition of the virtues. I am at the

The Ladder of John Climacus, Monastery of St Catherine, Sinai

summit of the ladder, and as my great initiate (St Paul) said: *"So faith, hope, love abide, these three; but the greatest of these is love (1 Cor 13: 13)!"* (30, 18; 1160).

At this point, a last question must be asked: can the *Ladder*, a work written by a hermit monk who lived 1,400 years ago, say something to us today? Can the existential journey of a man who lived his entire life on Mount Sinai in such a distant time be relevant to us? At first glance it would seem that the answer must be "no", because John Climacus is too remote from us. But if we look a little closer, we see that the monastic life is only a great symbol of baptismal life, of Christian life. It shows, so to speak, in capital letters what we write day after day in small letters. It is a prophetic symbol that reveals what the life of the baptised person is, in communion with Christ, with his death and Resurrection. The fact that the top of the "ladder", the final steps, are at the same time the fundamental, initial and most simple virtues is particularly important to me: faith, hope and charity. These are not virtues accessible only to moral heroes; rather they are gifts of God to all the baptised: in them our life develops too. The beginning is also the end, the starting point is also the point of arrival: the whole journey towards an ever more radical realisation of faith, hope and charity. The whole ascent is present in these virtues. Faith is fundamental, because this virtue implies that I renounce my arrogance, my thought, and the claim to judge by myself without entrusting myself to others. This journey towards humility, towards spiritual childhood is essential. It is necessary to overcome the attitude of arrogance that makes one say: I know better, in this my time of the 21st century, than what people could have known then. Instead, it is necessary to entrust oneself to Sacred Scripture alone, to the word of the Lord, to look out on the horizon of faith with humility, in order to enter into the enormous immensity of the universal world, of the world of God. In this way our soul grows, the sensitivity of the heart grows toward God. Rightly, John Climacus says that hope alone renders us capable of living charity; hope in which we transcend the things of every day, we do not expect success in our earthly days but we look forward to the revelation of God himself at last. It is only in this extension of our soul, in this self-transcendence, that our life becomes great and that we are able to bear the effort and disappointments of every day, that we can be kind to others without expecting any reward. Only if there is God, this great hope to which I aspire, can I take the small steps of my life and thus learn charity. The mystery of prayer, of the personal knowledge of Jesus, is concealed in charity: simple prayer that strives only to move the divine Teacher's heart. So it is that one's own heart opens, one learns from him his own kindness, his love. Let us therefore use this "ascent" of faith, hope and charity. In this way we will arrive at true life.

Bede the Venerable

Bede was born in the north-east of England, to be exact, Northumbria, in the year 672 or 673. He himself recounts that when he was seven years old his parents entrusted him to the Abbot of the neighbouring Benedictine monastery to be educated: "spending all the remaining time of my life a dweller in that monastery". He recalls, "I wholly applied myself to the study of Scripture; and amidst the observance of the monastic Rule and the daily charge of singing in church, I always took delight in learning, or teaching, or writing" (*Historia eccl. Anglorum*, v, 24). In fact, Bede became one of the most outstanding erudite figures of the early Middle Ages, since he was able to avail himself of many precious manuscripts which his Abbots would bring him on their return from frequent journeys to the continent and to Rome. His teaching and the fame of his writings occasioned his friendships with many of the most important figures of his time who encouraged him to persevere in his work from which so many were to benefit. When Bede fell ill, he did not stop

A scribe (probably Bede), miniature, *Life and miracles of St Cuthbert,* Add 39943, f. 2, British Library, London

working, always preserving an inner joy that he expressed in prayer and song. He ended his most important work, the *Historia Ecclesiastica gentis Anglorum*, with this invocation: "I beseech you, O good Jesus, that to the one to whom you have graciously granted sweetly to drink in the words of your knowledge, you will also vouchsafe in your loving kindness that he may one day come to you, the Fountain of all wisdom, and appear for ever before your face". Death took him on 26 May 737: it was the Ascension.

Sacred Scripture was the constant source of Bede's theological reflection. After a critical study of the text (a copy of the monumental *Codex Amiatinus* of the Vulgate on which Bede worked has come down to us), he comments on the Bible, interpreting it in a Christological key, that is, combining two things: on the one hand he listens to exactly what the text says, he really seeks to hear and understand the text itself; on the other, he is convinced that the key to understanding Sacred Scripture as the one word of God is Christ, and with Christ, in his light, one understands the Old and New Testaments as "one" Sacred Scripture. The events of the Old and New Testaments go together, they are the way to Christ, although expressed in different signs and institutions (this is what he calls the *concordia sacramentorum*). For example, the tent of the covenant that Moses pitched in the desert and the first and second temple of Jerusalem are images of the Church, the new temple built on Christ and on the Apostles with living stones, held together by the love of the Spirit. And just as pagan peoples also contributed to building the ancient temple by making available valuable materials and the technical experience of their master builders,

First page of the Venerable Bede's *Historia ecclesiastica gentis Anglorum*, Cott.Tib.C.II, f. 5v, historiated initial B with animal grotesques

Incipit
prefacio

Liber primus
ecclesiastice historiae
anglorum

Britannia oceani insula cui quondam Albion
nomen fuit inter septentrion-
alem ... est ... Germa-
niae ... Hispaniae ... maxi-
mis partibus ...

multo ... intervallo
... pmissa ... pars sit
cum longe lati-
... direptis dum
... rubus diversorum
... ium tractibus
quibus ...

... quadrin-
plecta; habet ...
... cuius ...
... meatibus ...
dictam ... por-
... civitatum
... occe-
ani post eo ma...
... milium ...
sive ... qui d...
... onum cccclx
... unde oce-
... optimae ...

so too contributing to the construction of the Church there were apostles and teachers, not only from ancient Jewish, Greek and Latin lineage, but also from the new peoples, among whom Bede was pleased to list the Irish Celts and Anglo-Saxons. St Bede saw the growth of the universal dimension of the Church which is not restricted to one specific culture but is comprised of all the cultures of the world that must be open to Christ and find in him their goal.

Another of Bede's favourite topics is the history of the Church. After studying the period described in the Acts of the Apostles, he reviews the history of the Fathers and the Councils, convinced that the work of the Holy Spirit continues in history. In the *Chronica Maiora*, Bede outlines a chronology that was to become the basis of the universal Calendar *"ab incarnatione Domini"*. In his day, time was calculated from the foundation of the City of Rome. Realising that the true reference point, the centre of history, is the Birth of Christ, Bede gave us this calendar that interprets history starting from the Incarnation of the Lord. Bede records the first six Ecumenical Councils and their developments, faithfully presenting Christian doctrine, both Mariological and soteriological, and denouncing the Monophysite and Monothelite, Iconoclastic and Neo-Pelagian heresies. Lastly he compiled with documentary rigour and literary expertise the *Ecclesiastical History of the English Peoples* mentioned above, which earned him recognition as "the father of English historiography". The characteristic features of the Church that Bede sought to emphasise are: a) *catholicity*, seen as faithfulness to tradition while remaining open to historical developments, and as the quest for unity in multiplicity, in historical and cultural diversity according to the directives Pope Gregory the Great had given to Augustine of Canterbury, the Apostle of

England; b) *apostolicity and Roman traditions:* in this regard he deemed it of prime importance to convince all the Irish, Celtic and Pict Churches to have one celebration for Easter in accordance with the Roman calendar. The *Computo*, which he worked out scientifically to establish the exact date of the Easter celebration, hence the entire cycle of the liturgical year, became the reference text for the whole Catholic Church.

Bede was also an eminent teacher of liturgical theology. In his Homilies on the Gospels for Sundays and feast days he achieves a true mystagogy, teaching the faithful to celebrate the mysteries of the faith joyfully and to reproduce them coherently in life, while awaiting their full manifestation with the return of Christ, when, with our glorified bodies, we shall be admitted to the offertory procession in the eternal liturgy of God in Heaven. Following the "realism" of the catecheses of Cyril, Ambrose and Augustine, Bede teaches that the sacraments of Christian initiation make every faithful person "not only a Christian but Christ". Indeed, every time that a faithful soul lovingly accepts and preserves the Word of God, in imitation of Mary, he conceives and generates Christ anew. And every time that a group of neophytes receives the Easter sacraments the Church "reproduces herself" or, to use a more daring term, the Church becomes "Mother of God", participating in the generation of her children through the action of the Holy Spirit.

By his way of creating theology, interweaving the Bible, liturgy and history, Bede has a timely message for the different "states of life": a) for scholars (*doctores ac doctrices*) he recalls two essential tasks: to examine the marvels of the word of God in order to present them in an attractive form to the faithful; to explain the dogmatic truths, avoiding heretical complications and keeping to "Catholic simplicity", with the attitude of the lowly and humble to whom God is pleased to reveal the mysteries of the Kingdom; b) pastors, for their part, must give priority to preaching, not only through verbal or hagiographic language but also by giving importance to icons, processions and pilgrimages. Bede recommends that they use the vulgate as he himself does, explaining the "Our Father" and the "Creed" in Northumbrian and continuing, until the last day of his life, his commentary on the Gospel of John in the vulgate; c) Bede recommends to consecrated people who devote themselves to the Divine Office, living in the joy of fraternal communion and progressing in the spiritual life by means of ascesis and contemplation that they attend to the apostolate no one possesses the Gospel for himself alone but must perceive it as a gift for others too both by collaborating with Bishops in pastoral activities of various kinds for the young Christian communities and by offering themselves for the evangelising mission among the pagans, outside their own country, as *"peregrini pro amore Dei"*.

Making this viewpoint his own, in his commentary on the Song of Songs Bede presents the Synagogue and the Church as collaborators in the dissemination of God's word. Christ the Bridegroom wants a hard-working Church, "weathered by the efforts of evangelisation" – there is a clear reference to the word in the Song of Songs (1: 5), where the bride says *"Nigra sum sed formosa"* (*"I am very dark, but comely"*) intent on tilling other fields or vineyards and in establishing among the new peoples "not a temporary hut but a permanent dwelling place", in other words, intent on integrating the Gospel into their social fabric and cultural institutions. In this perspective the holy Doctor urges lay faithful to be diligent in religious instruction, imitating those "insatiable crowds of the Gospel who did not even allow the Apostles time to take a mouthful". He teaches them how to pray ceaselessly, "reproducing in life what they celebrate in the liturgy", offering all their actions as a spiritual sacrifice in union with Christ. He explains to parents that in their small domestic circle too they can exercise "the priestly office as pastors and guides", giving their children a Christian upbringing. He also affirms that he knows many of the faithful (men and women, married and single) "capable of irreproachable conduct who, if appropriately guided, will be able every day to receive Eucharistic communion" (*Epist. ad Ecgberctum*, ed. Plummer, p. 419).

The fame of holiness and wisdom that Bede already enjoyed in his lifetime, earned him the title of "Venerable". Pope Sergius I called him this when he wrote to his Abbot in 701 asking him to allow him to come to Rome temporarily to give advice on matters of universal interest. After his death, Bede's writings were widely disseminated in his homeland and on the European continent. Bishop St Boniface, the great missionary of Germany, (d. 754), asked the Archbishop of York and the Abbot of Wearmouth several times to have some of his works transcribed and sent to him so that he and his companions might also enjoy the spiritual light that shone from them. A century later, Notker Balbulus, Abbot of Sankt Gallen (d. 912), noting the extraordinary influence of Bede, compared him to a new sun that God had caused to rise, not in the East but in the West, to illuminate the world. Apart from the rhetorical emphasis, it is a fact that with his works Bede made an effective contribution to building a Christian Europe in which the various peoples and cultures amalgamated with one another, thereby giving them a single physiognomy, inspired by the Christian faith. Let us pray that today too there may be figures of Bede's stature, to keep the whole continent united; let us pray that we may all be willing to rediscover our common roots, in order to be builders of a profoundly human and authentically Christian Europe.

ST·BONIFACE

Saint Boniface

A great eighth-century missionary who spread Christianity in Central Europe, indeed also in my own country: St Boniface has gone down in history as "the Apostle of the Germans". We have a fair amount of information on his life, thanks to the diligence of his biographers. He was born into an Anglo-Saxon family in Wessex in about 675 and was baptised with the name of Winfrid. He entered the monastery at a very early age, attracted by the monastic ideal. Since he possessed considerable intellectual ability, he seemed destined for a peaceful and brilliant academic career. He became a teacher of Latin grammar, wrote several treatises and even composed various poems in Latin. He was ordained a priest at the age of about 30 and felt called to an apostolate among the pagans on the continent. His country, Great Britain, which had been evangelised barely 100 years earlier by Benedictines led by St Augustine, at the time showed such sound faith and ardent charity that it could send missionaries to Central Europe to proclaim the Gospel there. In 716, Winfrid went to Frisia

Martyrdom of St Boniface, window, St Luke's Church Bath, England

(today Holland) with a few companions, but he encountered the opposition of the local chieftain and his attempt at evangelisation failed. Having returned home, he did not lose heart and two years later travelled to Rome to speak to Pope Gregory II and receive his instructions. One biographer recounts that the Pope welcomed him "with a smile and a look full of kindliness", and had "important conversations" with him in the following days (Willibaldo, [Willibald of Mainz], *Vita S. Bonifatii*, ed. Levison, pp. 13-14), and lastly, after conferring upon him the new name of Boniface, assigned to him, in official letters, the mission of preaching the Gospel among the German peoples.

Comforted and sustained by the Pope's support, Boniface embarked on the preaching of the Gospel in those regions, fighting against pagan worship and reinforcing the foundations of human and Christian morality. With a deep sense of duty he wrote in one of his letters: "We are united in the fight on the Lord's Day, because days of affliction and wretchedness have come... We are not mute dogs or taciturn observers or mercenaries fleeing from wolves! On the contrary, we are diligent Pastors who watch over Christ's flock, who proclaim God's will to the leaders and ordinary folk, to the rich and the poor... in season and out of season..." (cf. *Epistulae*, 3,352.354: MGH). With his tireless activity and his gift for organisation, Boniface adaptable and friendly yet firm, obtained great results. The Pope then "declared that he wished to confer upon him the episcopal dignity so that he might thus with greater determination correct and lead back to the path of truth those who had strayed, feeling supported by the greater authority of

Baptism and martyrdom of St Boniface, Msc.Lit.1, f. 126v, Staatsbibliothek, Bamberg

the apostolic dignity and being much more readily accepted by all in the office of preacher, the clearer it was that this was why he had been ordained by the Apostolic Bishop" (Othlo, *Vita S. Bonifatii*, ed. Levison, lib. I, p. 127).

The Supreme Pontiff himself consecrated Boniface "Regional Bishop" – that is, for the whole of Germany – Boniface then resumed his apostolic labours in the territories assigned to him and extended his action also to the Church of the Gauls: with great caution he restored discipline in the Church, convoked various Synods to guarantee the authority of the sacred canons and strengthened the necessary communion with the Roman Pontiff, a point that he had very much at heart. The Successors of Pope Gregory II also held him in the highest esteem. Gregory III appointed him Archbishop of all the Germanic tribes, sent him the pallium and granted him the faculties to organise the ecclesiastical hierarchy in those regions (cf. *Epist.* 28: *S. Bonifatii Epistulae*, ed. Tangl, Berolini 1916). Pope Zacchary confirmed him in his office and praised his dedication (cf. *Epist.* 51, 57, 58, 60, 68, 77, 80, 86, 87, 89: *op. cit.*); Pope Stephen III, newly elected, received a letter from him in which he expressed his filial respect (cf. *Epist.* 108: *op. cit.*).

In addition to this work of evangelisation and organisation of the Church through the founding of dioceses and the celebration of Synods, this great Bishop did not omit to encourage the foundation of various male and female monasteries so that they would become like beacons, so as to radiate human and Christian culture and the faith in the territory. He summoned monks and nuns from the Benedictine monastic communities in his homeland who gave him a most effective and invaluable help in proclaiming the Gospel and in disseminating the humanities and the arts among the population. Indeed, he rightly considered that work for the

Gospel must also be work for a true human culture. Above all the Monastery of Fulda – founded in about 743 – was the heart and centre of outreach of religious spirituality and culture: there the monks, in prayer, work and penance, strove to achieve holiness; there they trained in the study of the sacred and profane disciplines and prepared themselves for the proclamation of the Gospel in order to be missionaries. Thus it was to the credit of Boniface, of his monks and nuns – for women too had a very important role in this work of evangelisation – that human culture, which is inseparable from faith and reveals its beauty, flourished. Boniface himself has left us an important intellectual corpus. First of all is his copious correspondence, in which pastoral letters alternate with official letters and others more private in nature, which record social events but above all reveal his richly human temperament and profound faith.

In addition he composed a treatise on the *Ars grammatica* in which he explained the declinations, verbs and syntax of the Latin language, but which also became for him a means of spreading culture and the faith. An *Ars metrica*, that is an introduction on how to write poetry as well as various poetic compositions and, lastly, a collection of 15 sermons are also attributed to him.

Although he was getting on in years (he was almost 80), he prepared himself for a new evangelising mission: with about 50 monks he returned to Frisia where he had begun his work. Almost as a prediction of his imminent death, in alluding to the journey of life, he wrote to Bishop Lull, his disciple and successor in the see of Mainz: "I wish to bring to a conclusion the purpose of this journey; in no way can I renounce my desire to set out. The day of my end is near and the time of my death is approaching; having shed my mortal body, I shall rise to the

Des bertus saint bonisace enesque   IIII
Onsface fn home de biebono
zable qui tint leuesthie en

eternal reward. May you, my dear son, ceaselessly call the people from the maze of error, complete the building of the Basilica of Fulda that has already been begun, and in it lay my body, worn out by the long years of life" (Willibald, *Vita S. Bonifatii, ed. cit.,* p. 46). While he was beginning the celebration of Mass at Dokkum (in what today is northern Holland) on 5 June 754, he was assaulted by a band of pagans. Advancing with a serene expression he "forbade his followers from fighting saying, "cease, my sons, from fighting, give up warfare, for the witness of Scripture recommends that we do not give an eye for an eye but rather good for evil. Here is the long awaited day, the time of our end has now come; courage in the Lord!'" (*ibid.,* pp. 49-50). These were his last words before he fell under the blows of his aggressors. The mortal remains of the Martyr Bishop were then taken to the Monastery of Fulda where they received a fitting burial. One of his first biographers had already made this judgement of him: "The holy Bishop Boniface can call himself father of all the inhabitants of Germany, for it was he who first brought them forth in Christ with the words of his holy preaching, he strengthened them with his example and lastly, he gave his life for them; no greater love than this can be shown" (Othlo, *Vita S. Bonifatii, ed. cit.,* lib. I, p. 158).

Centuries later, what message can we gather today from the teaching and marvellous activity of this great missionary and martyr? For those who approach Boniface, an initial fact stands out: *the centrality of the word of God,* lived and interpreted in the faith of the Church, a word that he lived, preached and witnessed to until he gave the supreme gift of himself in martyrdom. He was so passionate about the word of God that he felt the urgent

St Boniface Archbishop of Mainz and St Venantius Foertunatus, miniature from *Le Miroir Historia* by Vincent de Beauvais, Musée Condé, Chantilly

need and duty to communicate it to others, even at his own personal risk. This word was the pillar of the faith which he had committed himself to spreading at the moment of his episcopal ordination: "I profess integrally the purity of the holy Catholic faith and with the help of God I desire to remain in the unity of this faith, in which there is no doubt that the salvation of Christians lies" (*Epist.* 12, in *S. Bonifatii Epistolae, ed. cit.,* p. 29). The second most important proof that emerges from the life of Boniface is his *faithful communion with the Apostolic See*, which was a firm and central reference point of his missionary work; he always preserved this communion as a rule of his mission and left it, as it were, as his will. In a letter to Pope Zachary, he said: "I never cease to invite and to submit to obedience to the Apostolic See those who desire to remain in the Catholic faith and in the unity of the Roman Church and all those whom God grants to me as listeners and disciples in my mission" (*Epist.* 50: in *ibid.,* p. 81). One result of this commitment was the steadfast spirit of cohesion around the Successor of Peter which Boniface transmitted to the Church in his mission territory, uniting England, Germany and France with Rome and thereby effectively contributing to planting those Christian roots of Europe which were to produce abundant fruit in the centuries to come. Boniface also deserves our attention for a third characteristic: he encouraged *the encounter between the Christian-Roman culture and the Germanic culture*. Indeed, he knew that humanising and evangelising culture was an integral part of his mission as Bishop. In passing on the ancient patrimony of Christian values, he grafted on to the Germanic populations a new, more human lifestyle, thanks to which the inalienable rights of the person were more widely respected. As a true son of St Benedict, he was able to combine prayer and labour (manual and intellectual), pen and plough.

Boniface's courageous witness is an invitation to us all to welcome God's word into our lives as an essential reference point, to love the Church passionately, to feel co-responsible for her future, to seek her unity around the Successor of Peter. At the same time, he reminds us that Christianity, by encouraging the dissemination of culture, furthers human progress. It is now up to us to be equal to such a prestigious patrimony and to make it fructify for the benefit of the generations to come.

His ardent zeal for the Gospel never fails to impress me. At the age of 41 he left a beautiful and fruitful monastic life, the life of a monk and teacher, in order to proclaim the Gospel to the simple, to barbarians; once again, at the age of 80, he went to a region in which he foresaw his martyrdom.

By comparing his ardent faith, this zeal for the Gospel, with our own often lukewarm and bureaucratised faith, we see what we must do and how to renew our faith, in order to give the precious pearl of the Gospel as a gift to our time.

ea sibi sub lieeaps suis do cece
a siaeiea beeaus do ce' aepts. hie u
lo luepes icheai sui monesteia

Ambrose Autpert

The Church lives in people and those who want to know the Church better, to understand her mystery, must consider the people who have seen and lived her message, her mystery. I have therefore been exploring people from whom we can learn what the Church is. We began with the Apostles and Fathers of the Church and we have gradually reached the eighth century, Charlemagne's period. Now I want to talk about Ambrose Autpert, a lesser known author; in fact, the majority of his works were attributed to other, better known people, from St Ambrose of Milan to St Ildefonsus, not to mention those that the monks of Monte Cassino claimed came from the pen of an abbot of theirs of the same name who lived almost a century later. Apart from a few brief autobiographical notes in his important commentary on the *Apocalypse*, we have little information about his life. Yet, an attentive reading of the works whose authorship the critic recognises makes it possible, little by little, to discover in his teaching a precious theological and spiritual treasure for our time too.

Abbot Ambrose Autpert receives a grant of land from the Emperor Charlemagne, miniature from the *Chronicon Vulturnense,* Cod.Barb.Lat. 2724 c. 66r, Vatican Library, Vatican City

Born into a noble family in Provence – according to his late biographer – Giovanni Ambrose Autpert was at the court of the Frankish King Pepin the Short where, in addition to his function as official, he somehow also played the role of tutor to the future Emperor Charlemagne. Autpert, probably in the retinue of Pope Stephen II, who in 753-54 went to the Frankish court, came to Italy and had the opportunity of visiting the famous Benedictine Abbey of St Vincent, located near the sources of the River Volturno in the Duchy of Benevento. Founded at the beginning of the century by three brothers from Benevento Paldone, Tatone and Tasone, the abbey was known as an oasis of classical and Christian culture. Shortly after his visit, Ambrose Autpert decided to embrace the religious life and entered that monastery where he acquired an appropriate education, especially in the fields of theology and spirituality, in accordance with the tradition of the Fathers. In about the year 761, he was ordained a priest and on 4 October 777 he was elected abbot with the support of the Frankish monks despite the opposition of the Lombards, who favoured Potone the Lombard. The nationalistic tension in the background did not diminish in the subsequent months. As a result, in the following year, 778, Autpert decided to resign and to seek shelter, together with several Frankish monks, in Spoleto where he could count on Charlemagne's protection. This, however, did not solve the dissension at St Vincent's Monastery. A few years later, when on the death of the abbot who had succeeded Autpert, Potone himself was elected as his successor (a. 782), the dispute flared up again and even led to the denunciation of the new abbot to Charlemagne. The latter sent the contenders to the tribunal of the Pontiff who summoned them to Rome. Autpert was also called as a witness. However, he died suddenly on the journey, perhaps murdered, on 30 January 784.

Ambrose Autpert was a monk and abbot in an epoch marked by strong political tensions which also had repercussions on life within the monasteries. We have frequent and disturbing echoes of them in his writings. He reports, for example, the contradiction between the splendid external appearance of monasteries and the tepidity of the monks: this criticism was also certainly directed at his own abbey. He wrote for his monastery the *Life* of the three founders with the clear intention of offering the new generation of monks a term of reference to measure up to. He also pursued a similar aim in a small ascetic treatise *Conflictus vitiorum et virtutum* ("Combat between the vices and the virtues"), which met with great acclaim in the Middle Ages and was published in 1473 in Utrecht, under Gregory the Great's name and, a year later, in Strasbourg under that of St Augustine. In it Ambrose Autpert intends to give the monks a practical training in how to face spiritual combat day after day. Significantly he applies the affirmation in 2 *Tim* 3: 12: "All who desire to live a godly life in Christ Jesus will be persecuted", no longer by external forces but by the assault that the Christian must face within him on the part of the forces of evil. Twenty-four pairs of fighters are presented in a sort of disputation: every vice seeks to lure the soul by subtle reasoning, whereas the respective virtue rebuffs these insinuations, preferably by using words of Scripture.

In this treatise on the combat between the vices and the virtues, Autpert sets *contemptus mundi* (contempt for the world) against *cupiditas* (greed) which becomes an important figure in the spirituality of monks. This contempt for the world is not a contempt for Creation, for the beauty and goodness of Creation and of the Creator, but a contempt for the false vision of the world that is presented to us and suggested to us precisely by covetousness. It insinuates that "having" is the supreme value of our being, of our life in the world, and seems important. And thus it falsifies the creation of the world and destroys the world. Autpert then remarks that the acquisitive greed of the rich and powerful in the society of his time also exists within the souls of monks and thus he writes a treatise entitled *De cupiditate*, in which, together with the Apostle Paul, he denounces greed from the outset as the root of all evil. He writes: "In the earth's soil various sharp thorns spring from different roots; in the human heart, on the other hand, the stings of all the vices sprout from a single root, greed" (*De cupiditate* 1: CCCM 27b, p. 963). In the light of the present global financial crisis, this report reveals its full timeliness. We see that it was precisely from this root of covetousness that the crisis sprang. Ambrose imagines the objection that the rich and powerful might raise, saying: but we are not monks, certain ascetic requirements do not apply to us. And he answers: "What you say is true, but for you, in the manner of your class and in accordance with your strength, the straight and narrow way applies because the Lord has proposed only two doors and two ways (that is, the narrow door and the wide door, the steep road and the easy one); he has not pointed to a third door or a third way" (*loc. cit.,* p. 978). He sees clearly that life-styles differ widely. Nonetheless the duty to combat greed, to fight the desire to possess, to appear, and the false concept of freedom as the faculty to dispose of all things as one pleases applies to the man in this world too and also to the rich. The rich person must also find the authentic road of truth, of love, and thus of an upright life. As a prudent pastor of souls, Autpert was thus able to speak a word of comfort at the end of his penitential homily: "I have not spoken against the greedy, but against greed, not against nature but against vice" (*loc. cit.,* p. 981).

Ambrose Autpert's most important work is without a doubt his commentary on the *Apocalypse* [*Expositio in Apocalypsim*] in 10 volumes: this constitutes, centuries later, the first broad commentary in the Latin world on the last book of Sacred Scripture. This work was the fruit of many years' work, carried out in two phases between 758 and 767, hence prior to his election as abbot. In the premise he is careful to indicate his sources, something that was not usual in the Middle Ages. Through what was perhaps his most significant source, the commentary of Bishop Primasius of Hadrumetum, written in about the middle of the sixth century, Autpert came into contact with the interpretation of the *Apocalypse* bequeathed to us by Ticonius, an African who lived a generation before St Augustine. He was not a Catholic; he belonged to the schismatic Donatist Church, yet he was a great theologian. In his commentary he sees the *Apocalypse* above all as a reflection of the mystery of the Church. Ticonius had reached the conviction that the Church was a bipartite body: on the one hand, he says, she belongs to Christ, but there is another part of the Church that belongs to the devil. Augustine read this commentary and profited from it but strongly emphasised that the Church is in Christ's hands, that she remains his Body, forming one with him, sharing in the mediation of grace. He therefore stresses that the Church can never be separated from Jesus Christ. In his interpretation of the *Apocalypse*, similar to that of Ticonius, Autpert is not so much concerned with the Second Coming of Christ at the end of time as rather with the

Double page spread: King Peppin offering the Monastery of Volturno in the person of St Vincent accompanied by Abbot Autpert and three monks, the income and lands of Penne and Aprutino, miniature from the Chronicon Vulturnense, Cod.Barb.Lat. 2724 c. 68v, Vatican Library, Vatican City

pinus filius Caroli magni
egis. longobardor. et in

N
HO
mine
Domi
ni de

...aluatoris nri ihu xpi. Pipinus

diuina elementia ordinante gsor

...regnans Francorum gentis rector.

...one pligendae ..., amilias ...

uncax ferzum Imperacatorc modefarm̄c
uniuf'oft preftacacf fubicumt abenaf
b fomc aug. Culum metabilf rept
rc ad hæcaf utbef pretartuf. ipinnifi

consequences that derive for the Church of the present from his First Coming, his Incarnation in the womb of the Virgin Mary. And he speaks very important words to us: in reality Christ "must be born, die and be raised daily in us, who are his Body" (*In Apoc.,* III: CCCM, 27, p. 205). In the context of the mystic dimension that invests every Christian he looks to Mary as a model of the Church, a model for all of us because Christ must also be born in and among us. Under the guidance of the Fathers, who saw the "woman clothed with the sun" of *Rv* 12: 1 as an image of the Church, Autpert argues: "the Blessed and devout Virgin... daily gives birth to new peoples from which the general Body of the Mediator is formed. It is therefore not surprising if she, in whose blessed womb the Church herself deserved to be united with her Head, represents the type of the Church". In this sense Autpert considers the Virgin Mary's role decisive in the work of the Redemption (cf. also his homilies *In purificatione S. Mariae* and *In adsumptione S. Mariae*). His great veneration and profound love for the Mother of God sometimes inspired in him formulations that in a certain way anticipated those of St Bernard and of Franciscan mysticism, yet without ever deviating to disputable forms of sentimentalism because he never separates Mary from the mystery of the Church. Therefore, with good reason, Ambrose Autpert is considered the first great Mariologist in the West. He considers that the profound study of the sacred sciences, especially meditation on the Sacred Scriptures, which he describes as "the ineffable sky, the unfathomable abyss" should be combined with the devotion that he believed must free the soul from attachment to earthly and transient pleasures (*In Apoc.* IX). In the beautiful prayer with which his commentary on the *Apocalypse* ends, underlining the priority that must be given to love in all theological research, he addresses God with these words: "When you are intellectually examined by us, you are not revealed as you truly are: when you are loved, you are attained".

Today we can see in Ambrose Autpert a personality who lived in a time of powerful political exploitation of the Church, in which nationalism and tribalism had disfigured the face of the Church. But he, in the midst of all these difficulties with which we too are familiar, was able to discover the true face of the Church in Mary, in the Saints, and he was thus able to understand what it means to be a Catholic, to be a Christian, to live on the word of God, to enter into this abyss and thus to live the mystery of the Mother of God: to give new life to the Word of God, to offer to the Word of God one's own flesh in the present time. And with all his theological knowledge, the depth of his knowledge, Autpert was able to understand that with merely theological research God cannot truly be known as he is. Love alone reaches him. Let us hear this message and pray the Lord to help us to live the mystery of the Church today in our time.

Germanus of Costantinople

Patriarch Germanus of Constantinople does not belong among the most representative figures of the Greek-speaking world of Eastern Christianity. Yet, his name appears with a certain solemnity in the list of the great champions of sacred images drafted by the Second Council of Nicaea, the seventh Ecumenical Council (787). The Greek Church celebrates his Feast in the liturgy of 12 May. He played an important role in the overall history of the controversy over images during the "Iconoclastic Crisis": he was able to resist effectively the pressures of an Iconoclast Emperor, in other words opposed to icons, such as Leo III.

During the patriarchate of Germanus (715-730) the capital of the Byzantine Empire, Constantinople, was subjected to a dangerous siege by the Saracens. On that occasion (717-718), a solemn procession was organised in the city displaying the image of the Mother of God, the *Theotokos*, and the relic of the True Cross, to invoke protection for the city from on high. In fact, Constantinople was liberated from the siege. The enemy

Germanus, Patriarch of Constantinople, fresco between central and southern apse, Cathedral of St Sofia, Novgorod

decided to desist for ever from the idea of establishing their capital in the city that was the symbol of the Christian Empire and the people were extremely grateful for the divine help.

After that event, Patriarch Germanus was convinced that God's intervention must be considered as obvious approval of the devotion shown by the people for the holy icons. However, the Emperor Leo III, was of the absolute opposite opinion; that very year (717) he was enthroned as the undisputed Emperor in the capital, over which he reigned until 741. After the liberation of Constantinople and after a series of other victories, the Christian Emperor began to show more and more openly his conviction that the consolidation of the Empire must begin precisely with a reordering of the manifestations of faith, with particular reference to the risk of idolatry to which, in his opinion, the people were prone because of their excessive worship of icons.

Patriarch Germanus' appeal to the tradition of the Church and to the effective efficacy of certain images unanimously recognised as "miraculous" were to no avail. The Emperor more and more stubbornly applied his restoration project which provided for the elimination of icons. At a public meeting on 7 January 730, when he openly took a stance against the worship of images, Germanus was in no way ready to comply with the Emperor's will on matters he himself deemed crucial for the Orthodox faith, of which he believed worship and love for images were part. As a consequence, Germanus was forced to resign from the office of Patriarch, condemning himself to exile in a monastery where he died forgotten by almost all. His name reappeared on the occasion of the Second Council of Nicaea (787), when the Orthodox Fathers decided in favour of icons, recognising the merits of Germanus.

Patriarch Germanus took great care of the liturgical celebrations and, for a certain time, was also believed to have introduced the feast of the *Akathistos*. As is well known, the *Akathistos* is a famous ancient hymn to the *Theotokos*, the Mother of God, that came into being in the Byzantine context. Despite the fact that from the theological viewpoint Germanus cannot be described as a great thinker, some of his works had a certain resonance, especially on account of some of his insights concerning *Mariology*. In fact, various of his homilies on Marian topics are extant, and some of them profoundly marked the piety of entire generations of faithful, both in the East and in the West. His splendid *Homilies on the Presentation of Mary at the Temple* are still living testimony of the unwritten tradition of the Christian Churches. Generations of nuns and monks and the members of a great number of institutes of consecrated life continue still today to find in these texts the most precious pearls of spirituality.

Some of Germanus' Mariological texts still give rise to wonder today. They are part of the homilies he gave *In SS. Deiparae dormitionem*, a celebration that corresponds with our Feast of the Assumption. Among these texts Pope Pius xii picked out one that he set like a pearl in his Apostolic Constitution *Munificentissimus Deus* (1950), with which he declared Mary's Assumption a Dogma of faith. Pope Pius XII cited this text in the above-mentioned Constitution, presenting it as one of the arguments in favour of the permanent faith of the Church concerning the bodily Assumption of Mary into Heaven. Germanus wrote: "May it never happen Most Holy Mother of God, that Heaven and earth, honoured by your presence, and you, with your departure, leave men and women without your protection? No. It is impossible to think of such things. In fact, just as when you were in the world you did not feel foreign to the realities of Heaven so too after you had emigrated from this world, you were not foreign to the possibility of communicating in spirit with mankind... You did not at all abandon those to whom you had guaranteed salvation... in fact, your spirit lives in eternity nor did your flesh suffer the corruption of the tomb. You, O Mother, are close to all and protect all, and although our eyes are unable to see you, we know, O Most Holy One, that you dwell among all of us and make yourself present in the most varied ways... You (Mary reveal your whole self, as is written, in your beauty. Your virginal body is entirely holy, entirely chaste, entirely the dwelling place of God so that, even for this reason, it is absolutely incorruptible. It is unchangeable since what was human in it has been taken up in incorruptibility, remaining alive and absolutely glorious, undamaged, and sharing in perfect life. Indeed, it was impossible that the one who had become the vase of God and the living temple of the most holy divinity of the Only Begotten One be enclosed in the sepulchre of the dead. On the other hand, we believe with certainty that you continue to walk with us" (*PG* 98, coll. 344B-346B, *passim*).

It has been said that for the Byzantines the decorum of the rhetorical form in preaching and especially in hymns or in the poetic compositions that they call *troparia* is equally important in the liturgical celebration as the beauty of the sacred building in which it takes place. Patriarch Germanus was recognised, in that tradition, as one who made a great contribution to keeping this conviction alive, that is, that the beauty of the words and language must coincide with the beauty of the building and the music.

Hymn to the Virgin Mary, miniature, Stories from the Old Testament and Illustrations of the Akathist Hymn and the twelve feasts, Benaki Museum, Athens

I quote, to conclude, the inspired words with which Germanus described the Church at the beginning of his small masterpiece: "The Church is the temple of God, a sacred space, a house of prayer, the convocation of people, the Body of Christ... She is Heaven on earth where the transcendent God dwells as if in his own home and passes through, but she is also an impression made (*antitypos*) of the Crucifixion, the tomb and the Resurrection... The Church is God's house in which the life-giving mystical sacrifice is celebrated, at the same time the most intimate part of the shrine and sacred grotto. Within her in fact the sepulchre and the table are found, nourishment for the soul and a guarantee of life. In her, lastly, are found those true and proper precious pearls which are the divine dogmas of teaching that the Lord offered directly to this disciples" (*PG* 98, coll. 384B-385A).

Lastly, the question remains: what does this Saint chronologically and also culturally rather distant from us have to tell us today? I am thinking mainly of three things. The first: there is a certain visibility of God in the world, in the Church, that we must learn to perceive. God has created man in his image, but this image was covered with the scum of so much sin that God almost no longer shines through it. Thus the Son of God was made true man, a perfect image of God: thus in Christ we may also contemplate the Face of God and learn to be true men ourselves, true images of God. Christ invites us to imitate him, to become similar to him, so in every person the Face of God shines out anew. To tell the truth, in the Ten Commandments God forbade the making of images of God, but this was because of the temptations to idolatry to which the believer might be exposed in a context of paganism. Yet when God made himself visible in Christ through the Incarnation, it became legitimate to reproduce the Face of Christ. The holy images teach us to see God represented in the Face of Christ. After the Incarnation of the Son of God, it therefore became possible to see God in images of Christ and also in the faces of the Saints, in the faces of all people in whom God's holiness shines out.

The second thing is the beauty and dignity of the liturgy. To celebrate the liturgy in the awareness of God's presence, with that dignity and beauty which make a little of his splendour visible, is the commitment of every Christian trained in his faith. The third thing is to love the Church. Precisely with regard to the Church, we men and women are prompted to see above all the sins and the negative side, but with the help of faith, which enables us to see in an authentic way, today and always we can rediscover the divine beauty in her. It is in the Church that God is present, offers himself to us in the Holy Eucharist and remains present for adoration. In the Church God speaks to us, in the Church God "walks beside us" as St Germanus said. In the Church we receive God's forgiveness and learn to forgive.

Let us pray God to teach us to see his presence and his beauty in the Church, to see his presence in the world and to help us too to be transparent to his light.

Double page spread: *Akathist Hymn to the Virgin Mary*, detail of fresco from Humor Monastery, Bucovina, Romania

John Damascene

John Damascene was a personage of prime importance in the history of Byzantine Theology, a great Doctor in the history of the Universal Church. Above all he was an eyewitness of the passage from the Greek and Syrian Christian cultures shared by the Eastern part of the Byzantine Empire, to the Islamic culture, which spread through its military conquests in the territory commonly known as the Middle or Near East. John, born into a wealthy Christian family, at an early age assumed the role, perhaps already held by his father, of Treasurer of the Caliphate. Very soon, however, dissatisfied with life at court, he decided on a monastic life, and entered the monastery of Mar Saba, near Jerusalem. This was around the year 700. He never again left the monastery, but dedicated all his energy to ascesis and literary work, not disdaining a certain amount of pastoral activity, as is shown by his numerous homilies. His liturgical commemoration is on the 4 December. Pope Leo XIII proclaimed him Doctor of the Universal Church in 1890.

Saints John Climacus, John Damascene and Arsenius,
detail of John Damascene, Novgorod Museum

In the East, his best remembered works are the three *Discourses against those who calumniate the Holy Images*, which were condemned after his death by the iconoclastic Council of Hieria (754). These discourses, however, were also the fundamental grounds for his rehabilitation and canonisation on the part of the Orthodox Fathers summoned to the Council of Nicaea (787), the Seventh Ecumenical Council. In these texts it is possible to trace the first important theological attempts to legitimise the veneration of sacred images, relating them to the mystery of the Incarnation of the Son of God in the womb of the Virgin Mary.

John Damascene was also among the first to distinguish, in the cult, both public and private, of the Christians, between worship (*latreia*), and veneration (*proskynesis*): the first can only be offered to God, spiritual above all else, the second, on the other hand, can make use of an image to address the one whom the image represents. Obviously the Saint can in no way be identified with the material of which the icon is composed. This distinction was immediately seen to be very important in finding an answer in Christian terms to those who considered universal and eternal the strict Old Testament prohibition against the use of cult images. This was also a matter of great debate in the Islamic world, which accepts the Jewish tradition of the total exclusion of cult images. Christians, on the other hand, in this context, have discussed the problem and found a justification for the veneration of images. John Damascene writes, "In other ages God had not been represented in images, being incorporate and faceless. But since God has now been seen in the flesh, and lived among men, I represent that part of God which is visible. I do not venerate matter, but the Creator of matter, who became matter for my sake and deigned to live in matter and bring about my salvation through matter. I will not cease therefore to venerate that matter through which my salvation was achieved. But I do not venerate it in absolute terms as God! How could that which, from non-existence, has been given existence, be God?... But I also venerate and respect all the rest of matter which has brought me salvation, since it is full of energy and Holy graces. Is not the wood of the Cross, three times blessed, matter?... And the ink, and the most Holy Book of the Gospels, are they not matter? The redeeming altar which dispenses the Bread of life, is it not matter?... And, before all else, are not the flesh and blood of Our Lord matter? Either we must suppress the sacred nature of all these things, or we must concede to the tradition of the Church the veneration of the images of God and that of the friends of God who are sanctified by the name they bear, and for this reason are possessed by the grace of the Holy Spirit. Do not, therefore, offend matter: it is not contemptible, because nothing that God has made is contemptible" (cf. *Contra imaginum calumniatores*, I, 16, ed. Kotter, pp. 89-90). We see that as a result of the Incarnation, matter is seen to have become divine, is seen as the habitation of God. It is a new vision of the world and of material reality. God became flesh and flesh became truly the habitation of God, whose glory shines in the human Face of Christ. Thus the arguments of the Doctor of the East are still extremely relevant today, considering the very great dignity that matter has acquired through the Incarnation, capable of becoming, through faith, a sign and a sacrament, efficacious in the meeting of man with God. John Damascene remains, therefore, a privileged witness of the cult of icons, which would come to be one of the most distinctive aspects of Eastern spirituality up to the present day. It is, however, a form of cult which belongs simply to the Christian faith, to the faith in that God who became flesh and was made visible. The teaching of Saint John Damascene thus finds its place in the tradition of the universal Church, whose sacramental doctrine foresees that material elements taken from nature can become vehicles of grace by virtue of the invocation (*epiclesis*) of the Holy Spirit, accompanied by the confession of the true faith.

John Damascene extends these fundamental ideas to the veneration of the relics of Saints, on the basis of the conviction that the Christian Saints, having become partakers of the Resurrection of Christ, cannot be considered simply "dead". Numbering, for example, those whose relics or images are worthy of veneration, John states in his third discourse in defence of images: "First of all (let us venerate) those among whom God reposed, he alone Holy, who reposes among the Saints (cf. *Is* 57: 15), such as the Mother of God and all the Saints. These are those who, as far as possible, have made themselves similar to God by their own will; and by God's presence in them, and his help, they are really called gods (cf. *Ps* 82[81]: 6), not by their nature, but by contingency, just as the red-hot iron is called fire, not by its nature, but by contingency and its participation in the fire. He says in fact : you shall be holy, because I am Holy (cf. *Lv* 19: 2)" (III, 33, col. 1352 a). After a series of references of this kind, John Damascene was able serenely to deduce: "God, who is good, and greater than any goodness, was not content with the contemplation of himself, but desired that there should be beings benefited by him, who might share in his goodness: therefore he created from nothing all things, visible and invisible, including man, a reality visible and invisible. And he created him envisaging him and creating him as a being capable

Dream of St John Damascene, miniature from *Le Miroir Historia* by Vincent de Beauvais, Musée Condé, Chantilly

Estui saint patriarche∙siconce il
mesmes liraconte estoit encores
iennec encthupre de seaige de vb
ans∙ Il bit une nuit envision une pucelle
elle plus Resplandissant que se soulcil
et aournee tres clerement qui setent denar
son lit et le bouta ou couste et qnant il su
esueille il la bit brayement et tuida que
ce sust une semme car elle auoit une cou
ronne sur son chief qni estoit de trinite
dolinet et il se semedia du signe de lacroy
et lui dist qni es tu et coment osac tu en
tier sur moy auant te dozmoyre et elle lui

of thought (*ennoema ergon*), enriched with the word (*logo[i] symploroumenon*), and orientated towards the spirit (*pneumati teleioumenon*)" (II, 2, pg 94, col. 865a). And to clarify this thought further, he adds: "We must allow ourselves to be filled with wonder (*thaumazein*) at all the works of Providence (*tes pronoias erga*), to accept and praise them all, overcoming any temptation to identify in them aspects which to many may seem unjust or iniquitous, (*adika*), and admitting instead that the project of God (*pronoia*) goes beyond man's capacity to know or to understand (*agnoston kai akatalepton*), while on the contrary only he may know our thoughts, our actions, and even our future" (ii, 29, pg 94, col. 964c). Plato had in fact already said that all philosophy begins with wonder. Our faith, too, begins with wonder at the very fact of the Creation, and at the beauty of God who makes himself visible.

The optimism of the contemplation of nature (*physike theoria*), of seeing in the visible creation the good, the beautiful, the true, this Christian optimism, is not ingenuous: it takes account of the wound inflicted on human nature by the freedom of choice desired by God and misused by man, with all the consequences of widespread discord which have derived from it. From this derives the need, clearly perceived by John Damascene, that nature, in which the goodness and beauty of God are reflected, wounded by our fault, "should be strengthened and renewed" by the descent of the Son of God in the flesh, after God had tried in many ways and on many occasions, to show that he had created man so that he might exist not only in "being", but also in "well-being" (cf. *The Orthodox Faith*, II, 1, pg 94, col. 981). With passionate eagerness John explains: "It was necessary for nature to be strengthened and renewed, and for the path of virtue to be indicated and effectively taught (*didachthenai aretes hodòn*), the path that leads away from corruption and towards eternal life... So there appeared on the horizon of history the great sea of love that God bears towards man (*philanthropias pelagos*)... It is a fine expression. We see on one side the beauty of Creation, and on the other the destruction wrought by the fault of man. But we see in the Son of God, who descends to renew nature, the sea of love that God has for man. John Damascene continues: "He himself, the Creator and the Lord, fought for his Creation, transmitting to it his teaching by example... And so the Son of God, while still remaining in the form of God, lowered the skies and descended... to his servants... achieving the newest thing of all, the only thing really new under the sun, through which he manifested the infinite power of God" (III, 1, pg 94, col. 981c-984b).

We may imagine the comfort and joy which these words, so rich in fascinating images, poured into the hearts of the faithful. We listen to them today, sharing the same feelings with the Christians of those far-off days: God desires to repose in us, he wishes to renew nature through our conversion, he wants to allow us to share in his divinity. May the Lord help us to make these words the substance of our lives.

St John Damascene and the lion, fresco, Hagios Pandes Monastery, Areopolis, Greece

Saint Theodore the Studite

St Theodore the Studite, brings us to the middle of the medieval Byzantine period, in a somewhat turbulent period from the religious and political perspectives. St Theodore was born in 759 into a devout noble family: his mother Theoctista and an uncle, Plato, Abbot of the Monastery of Saccudium in Bithynia, are venerated as saints. Indeed it was his uncle who guided him towards monastic life, which he embraced at the age of 22. He was ordained a priest by Patriarch Tarasius, but soon ended his relationship with him because of the toleration the Patriarch showed in the case of the adulterous marriage of the Emperor Constantine VI. This led to Theodore's exile in 796 to Thessalonica. He was reconciled with the imperial authority the following year under the Empress Irene, whose benevolence induced Theodore and Plato to transfer to the urban monastery of Studios, together with a large portion of the community of the monks of Saccudium, in order to avoid the Saracen incursions. So it was that the important "Studite Reform" began.

St Theodore the Studite, Mosaic, Nea Moni Monastery, Chios, Greece

Theodore's personal life, however, continued to be eventful. With his usual energy, he became the leader of the resistance against the iconoclasm of Leo V, the Armenian who once again opposed the existence of images and icons in the Church. The procession of icons organised by the monks of Studios evoked a reaction from the police. Between 815 and 821, Theodore was scourged, imprisoned and exiled to various places in Asia Minor. In the end he was able to return to Constantinople but not to his own monastery. He therefore settled with his monks on the other side of the Bosporus. He is believed to have died in Prinkipo on 11 November 826, the day on which he is commemorated in the Byzantine Calendar. Theodore distinguished himself within Church history as one of the great reformers of monastic life and as a defender of the veneration of sacred images, beside St Nicephorus, Patriarch of Constantinople, in the second phase of the iconoclasm.

Theodore had realised that the issue of the veneration of icons was calling into question the truth of the Incarnation itself. In his three books, the *Antirretikoi* (*Confutations*), Theodore makes a comparison between eternal intra-Trinitarian relations, in which the existence of each of the divine Persons does not destroy their unity, and the relations between Christ's two natures, which do not jeopardise in him the one Person of the *Logos*. He also argues: abolishing veneration of the icon of Christ would mean repudiating his redeeming work, given that, in assuming human nature, the invisible eternal *Word* appeared in visible human flesh and in so doing sanctified the entire visible cosmos.

Theodore and his monks, courageous witnesses in the period of the iconoclastic persecutions, were inseparably bound to the reform of coenobitic life in the Byzantine world. Their importance was notable if only for an external circumstance: their number. Whereas the number of monks in monasteries of that time did not exceed 30 or 40, we know from the *Life of Theodore* of the existence of more than 1,000 Studite monks overall. Theodore himself tells us of the presence in his monastery of about 300 monks; thus we see the enthusiasm of faith that was born within the context of this man's being truly informed and formed by faith itself. However, more influential than these numbers was the new spirit the Founder impressed on coenobitic life. In his writings, he insists on the urgent need for a conscious return to the teaching of the Fathers, especially to St Basil, the first legislator of monastic life, and to St Dorotheus of Gaza, a famous spiritual Father of the Palestinian desert. Theodore's characteristic contribution consists in insistence on the need for order and submission on the monks' part. During the persecutions they had scattered and each one had grown accustomed to living according to his own judgement. Then, as it was possible to re-establish community life, it was necessary to do the utmost to make the monastery once again an organic community, a true family, or, as St Theodore said, a true "Body of Christ". In such a community the reality of the Church as a whole is realised concretely.

Another of St Theodore's basic convictions was this: monks, differently from lay people, take on the commitment to observe the Christian duties with greater strictness and intensity. For this reason they make a special profession which belongs to the *hagiasmata* (*consecrations*), and it is, as it were, a "new Baptism", symbolised by their taking the habit. Characteristic of monks in comparison with lay people, then, is the commitment to poverty, chastity and obedience. In addressing his monks, Theodore spoke in a practical, at times picturesque manner about poverty, but poverty in the following of Christ is from the start an essential element of monasticism and also points out a way for all of us. The renunciation of private property, this freedom from material things, as well as moderation and simplicity apply in a radical form only to monks, but the spirit of this renouncement is equal for all. Indeed, we must not depend on material possessions but instead must learn renunciation, simplicity, austerity and moderation. Only in this way can a supportive society develop and the great problem of poverty in this world be overcome. Therefore, in this regard the monks' radical poverty is essentially also a path for us all. Then when he explains the temptations against chastity, Theodore does not conceal his own experience and indicates the way of inner combat to find self control and hence respect for one's own body and for the body of the other as a temple of God.

However, the most important renunciations in his opinion are those required by obedience, because each one of the monks has his own way of living, and fitting into the large community of 300 monks truly involves a new way of life which he describes as the "martyrdom of submission". Here too the monks' example serves to show us how necessary this is for us, because, after the original sin, man has tended to do what he likes. The first principle is for the life of the world, all the rest must be subjected to it. However, in this way, if each person is self-centred, the social structure cannot function. Only by learning to fit into the common freedom, to share and to submit to it, learning legality, that is, submission and obedience to the rules of the common good and life in common, can society be healed, as well as the *self*, of the pride of being the centre of the world. Thus St Theodore, with fine introspection, helped his monks and ultimately also helps us to understand true life, to resist the temptation to set up our own will as the supreme rule of life and to preserve our true personal identity which is always an identity shared with others and peace of heart.

For Theodore the Studite an important virtue on a par with obedience and humility is *philergia*, that is, the love of work, in which he sees a criterion by which to judge the quality of personal devotion: the person who is fervent and works hard in material concerns, he argues, will be the same in those of the spirit. Therefore he does not permit the monk to dispense with work, including manual work, under the pretext of prayer and contemplation; for work to his mind and in the whole monastic tradition is actually a means of finding God. Theodore is not afraid to speak of work as the "sacrifice of the monk", as his "liturgy", even as a sort of Mass through which monastic life becomes angelic life. And it is precisely in this way that the world of work must be humanised and man, through work, becomes more himself and closer to God. One consequence of this unusual vision is worth remembering: precisely because it is the fruit of a form of "liturgy", the riches obtained from common work must not serve for the monks' comfort but must be earmarked for assistance to the poor. Here we can all understand the need for the proceeds of work to be a good for all. Obviously the "Studites'" work was not only manual: they had great importance in the religious and cultural development of the Byzantine civilisation as calligraphers, painters, poets, educators of youth, school teachers and librarians.

Although he exercised external activities on a truly vast scale, Theodore did not let himself be distracted from what he considered closely relevant to his role as superior: being the spiritual father of his monks. He knew what a crucial influence both his good mother and his holy uncle Plato whom he described with the significant title "father" had had on his life. Thus he himself provided spiritual direction for the monks. Every day, his biographer says, after evening prayer he would place himself in front of the iconostasis to listen to the confidences of all. He also gave spiritual advice to many people outside the monastery. The *Spiritual Testament* and the *Letters* highlight his open and affectionate character, and show that true spiritual friendships were born from his fatherhood both in the monastic context and outside it.

The *Rule*, known by the name of *Hypotyposis*, codified shortly after Theodore's death, was adopted, with a few modifications, on Mount Athos when in 962 St Athanasius Anthonite founded the Great Laura there, and in the Kievan Rus', when at the beginning of the second millennium St Theodosius introduced it into the Laura of the Grottos. Understood in its genuine meaning, the *Rule* has proven to be unusually up to date. Numerous trends today threaten the unity of the common faith and impel people towards a sort of dangerous spiritual individualism and spiritual pride. It is necessary to strive to defend and to increase the perfect unity of the Body of Christ, in which the peace of order and sincere personal relations in the Spirit can be harmoniously composed.

It may be useful to return at the end to some of the main elements of Theodore's spiritual doctrine: love for the Lord incarnate and for his visibility in the Liturgy and in icons; fidelity to Baptism and the commitment to live in communion with the Body of Christ, also understood as the communion of Christians with each other; a spirit of poverty, moderation and renunciation; chastity, self-control, humility and obedience against the primacy of one's own will that destroys the social fabric and the peace of souls; love for physical and spiritual work; spiritual love born from the purification of one's own conscience, one's own soul, one's own life. Let us seek to comply with these teachings that really do show us the path of true life.

Rabanus Maurus

In this chapter I would like to speak of a truly extraordinary figure of the Latin West: Rabanus Maurus, a monk. Together with men such as Isidore of Seville, the Venerable Bede and Ambrose Autpert of whom I have already spoken, during the centuries of the so-called "High Middle Ages" he was able to preserve the contact with the great culture of the ancient scholars and of the Christian Fathers. Often remembered as the *"praeceptor Germaniae"*, Rabanus Maurus was extraordinarily prolific. With his absolutely exceptional capacity for work, he perhaps made a greater contribution than anyone else to keeping alive that theological, exegetic and spiritual culture on which successive centuries were to draw. He was referred to by great figures belonging to the monastic world such as Peter Damian, Peter the Venerable and Bernard of Clairvaux, as well as by an ever increasing number of *"clerics"* of the secular clergy who gave life to one of the most beautiful periods of the fruitful flourishing of human thought in the 12th and 13th centuries.

Rabanus Maurus offering his book to Pope Gregory I, miniature, Ms. 340/1, f. 39v, Bibliothèque Municipale, Douai, France

Born in Mainz in about 780, Rabanus entered the monastery at a very early age. He was nicknamed "Maurus" after the young St Maur who, according to *Book II of the Dialogues* of St Gregory the Great, was entrusted by his parents, Roman nobles, to the Abbot Benedict of Norcia. Alone this precocious insertion of Rabanus as *"puer oblatus"* in the Benedictine monastic world and the benefits he drew from it for his own human, cultural and spiritual growth, were to provide an interesting glimpse not only of the life of monks and of the Church, but also of the whole of society of his time, usually described as "Carolingian". About them or perhaps about himself, Rabanus Maurus wrote: "There are some who have had the good fortune to be introduced to the knowledge of Scripture from a tender age (*"a cunabulis suis"*) and who were so well-nourished with the food offered to them by Holy Church as to be fit for promotion, with the appropriate training, to the highest of sacred Orders" (*PL* 107, col. 419 BC).

The extraordinary culture for which Rabanus Maurus was distinguished soon brought him to the attention of the great of his time. He became the advisor of princes. He strove to guarantee the unity of the Empire and, at a broader cultural level, never refused to give those who questioned him a carefully considered reply, which he found preferably in the Bible or in the texts of the Holy Fathers. First elected Abbot of the famous Monastery of Fulda and then appointed Archbishop of Mainz, his native city, this did not stop him from pursuing his studies, showing by the example of his life that it is possible to be at the same time available to others without depriving oneself of the appropriate time for reflection, study and meditation. Thus Rabanus Maurus was exegete, philosopher, poet, pastor and man of God. The Dioceses of Fulda, Mainz, Limburg and Breslau (Wrocław) venerate him as a saint or blessed. His works fill at least six volumes of Migne's *Patrologia Latina*. It is likely that we are indebted to him for one of the most beautiful hymns known to the Latin Church, the *"Veni Creator Spiritus"*, an extraordinary synthesis of Christian pneumatology. In fact, Rabanus' first theological work is expressed in the form of poetry and had as its subject the mystery of the Holy Cross in a book entitled: *"De laudibus Sanctae Crucis"*, conceived in such a way as to suggest not only a conceptual content but also more exquisitely artistic stimuli, by the use of both poetic and pictorial forms within the same manuscript codex. Suggesting the image of the Crucified Christ between the lines of his writing, he says, for example: "This is the image of the Saviour who, with the position of his limbs, makes sacred for us the most salubrious, gentle and loving form of the Cross, so that by believing in his Name and obeying his commandments we may obtain eternal life thanks to his Passion. However, every time we raise our eyes to the Cross, let us remember the one who died for us to save us from the powers of darkness, accepting death to make us heirs to eternal life" (*Lib.* 1, fig. 1, *PL* 107 col. 151 C).

This method of combining all the arts, the intellect, the heart and the senses, which came from the East, was to experience a great development in the West, reaching unparalleled heights in the miniature codices of the Bible and in other works of faith and art that flourished in Europe until the invention of printing and beyond. In Rabanus Maurus, in any case, is shown an extraordinary awareness of the need to involve, in the experience of faith, not only the mind and the heart, but also the senses through those other aspects of aesthetic taste and human sensitivity that lead man to benefit from the truth with his whole self, "mind, soul and body". This is important: faith is not only thought but also touches the whole of our being. Since God became Man in flesh and blood, since he entered the tangible world, we must seek and encounter God in all the dimensions of our being. Thus the reality of God, through faith, penetrates our being and transforms it. This is why Rabanus Maurus focused his attention above all on the Liturgy as a synthesis of all the dimensions of our perception of reality. This intuition of Rabanus Maurus makes it extraordinarily up to date. Also famous among his opus are the *"Hymns"*, suggested for use especially in liturgical celebrations. In fact, since Rabanus was primarily a monk, his interest in the liturgical celebration was taken for granted. However, he did not devote himself to the art of poetry as an end in itself but, rather, used art and every other form of erudition as a means for deepening knowledge of the word of God. He therefore sought with great application and rigour to introduce his contemporaries, especially ministers (Bishops, priests and deacons), to an understanding of the profoundly theological and spiritual meaning of all the elements of the liturgical celebration.

He thus sought to understand and to present to others the theological meanings concealed in the rites, drawing from the Bible and from the tradition of the Fathers. For the sake of honesty and to give greater weight to his explanations, he did not hesitate to indicate the Patristic sources to which he owed his knowledge. Nevertheless he used them with freedom and with careful discernment, continuing the development of patristic thought. At the end of the *"Epistola prima"*, addressed to a "chorbishop" of the Diocese of Mainz, for example, after answering the requests for clarification concerning the

Finger counting from 1 to 20,000, miniature from *De numeris* by Rabanus Maurus. Codex *Alcobacense*, f. 251v, Istituto da Biblioteca Nacional, Lisbon

dufis. dipondf. treffis. quadra
fis. quinquis. fexis. Septufis.
octufis. et c e ꝛ e ꝛa.

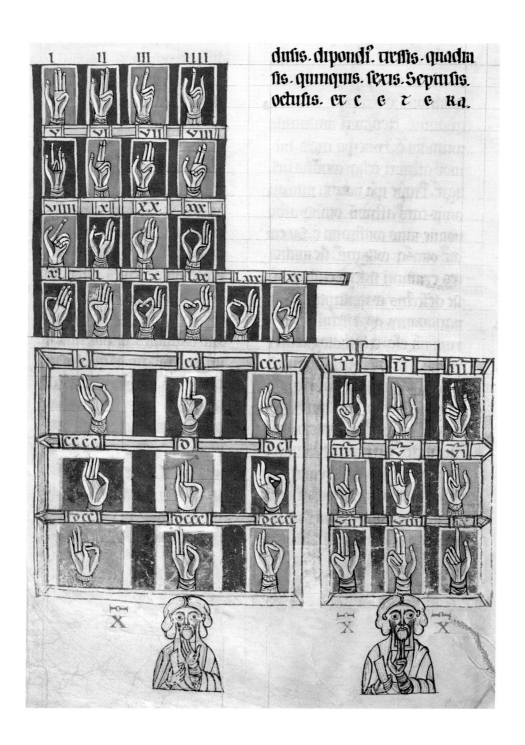

79

behaviour to adopt in the exercise of pastoral responsibility, he continues, "We have written all these things for you as we deduced them from the Sacred Scriptures and the canons of the Fathers. Yet, most holy man, may you take your decisions as you think best, case by case, seeking to temper your evaluation in such a way as to guarantee discretion in all things because it is the mother of all the virtues" (*Epistulae*, I, *PL* 112, col. 1510 C). Thus the continuity of the Christian faith which originates in the word of God becomes visible; yet it is always alive, develops and is expressed in new ways, ever consistent with the whole construction, with the whole edifice of faith.

Since an integral part of liturgical celebration is the word of God Rabanus Maurus dedicated himself to it with the greatest commitment throughout his life. He produced appropriate exegetic explanations for almost all the biblical books of the Old and New Testament, with clearly pastoral intentions that he justified with words such as these: "I have written these things... summing up the explanations and suggestions of many others, not only in order to offer a service to the poor reader, who may not have many books at his disposal, but also to make it easier for those who in many things do not succeed in entering in depth into an understanding of the meanings discovered by the Fathers" (*Commentariorum in Matthaeum praefatio, PL* 107, col. 727 D). In fact, in commenting on the biblical texts he drew amply from the ancient Fathers, with special preference for Jerome, Ambrose, Augustine and Gregory the Great.

His outstanding pastoral sensitivity later led him to occupy himself above all with one of the problems most acutely felt by the faithful and sacred ministers of his time: that of Penance. Indeed, he compiled the *"Penitenziari"* – this is what he called them – in which, according to the sensibility of his day, sins and the corresponding punishments were listed, using as far as possible reasons found in the Bible, in the decisions of the Councils and in Papal Decretals. The "Carolingians" also used these texts in their attempt to reform the Church and society. Corresponding with the same pastoral intentions, were works such as *"De disciplina ecclesiastica"* and *"De institutione clericorum"*, in which, drawing above all from Augustine, Rabanus explained to the simple and to the clergy of his diocese the basic elements of the Christian faith: they were like little catechisms.

I would like to end the presentation of this great "churchman" by quoting some of his words in which his basic conviction is clearly reflected: "Those who are negligent in contemplation *("qui vacare Deo negligit")*, deprive themselves of the vision of God's light; then those who let themselves be indiscreetly invaded by worries and allow their thoughts to be overwhelmed by the tumult of worldly things condemn themselves to the absolute impossibility of penetrating the secrets of the invisible God" (*Lib* I, *PL* 112, col. 1263 A). I think that Rabanus Maurus is also addressing these words to us today: in periods of work, with its frenetic pace, and in holiday periods we must reserve moments for God. We must open our lives to him, addressing to him a thought, a reflection, a brief prayer, and above all we must not forget Sunday as the Lord's Day, the day of the Liturgy, in order to perceive God's beauty itself in the beauty of our churches, in our sacred music and in the word of God, letting him enter our being. Only in this way does our life become great, become true life.

IOHANNES·SCOTVS·

John Scotus Erigena

In this chapter I would like to explore a noteworthy thinker of the Christian West: John Scotus Erigena, whose origins are nonetheless obscure. He certainly came from Ireland, where he was born at the beginning of the ninth century, but we do not know when he left his Island to cross the Channel and thus fully enter that cultural world which was coming into being around the Carolingians, and in particular around Charles the Bald, in ninth-century France. Just as we are not certain of the date of his birth, likewise we do not know the year of his death but, according to the experts, it must have been in about the year 870.

John Scotus Erigena had a patristic culture, both Greek and Latin, at first hand. Indeed, he had direct knowledge of the writings of both the Latin and the Greek Fathers. He was well acquainted, among others, with the works of Augustine, Ambrose, Gregory the Great and the important Fathers of the Christian West, but he was just as familiar with the thought of Origen, Gregory of Nyssa, John Chrysostom and other Christian Fathers of the East who were equally important. He was an exceptional man who in that period had also mastered

John Scotus Erigena, inlaid wood mosaic, St Francis, Assisi the Greek language. He devoted very special attention to St Maximus Confessor and above all to Dionysius the Areopagite. This pseudonym conceals a fifth-century ecclesiastical writer, but throughout the Middle Ages people, including John Scotus Erigena, were convinced that this author could be identified with a direct disciple of St Paul who is mentioned in the Acts of the Apostles (17: 34). Scotus Erigena, convinced of the apostolicity of Dionysius' writings, described him as a "divine author" par excellence; Dionysius' writings were therefore an eminent source of his thought. John Scotus translated his works into Latin. The great medieval theologians, such as St Bonaventure, became acquainted with Dionysius' works through this translation. Throughout his life John Scotus devoted himself to deepening his knowledge and developing his thought, drawing on these writings, to the point that still today it can sometimes be difficult to distinguish where we are dealing with Scotus Erigena's thought and where, instead, he is merely proposing anew the thought of Pseudo-Dionysius.

The theological opus of John Scotus truly did not meet with much favour. Not only did the end of the Carolingian era cause his works to be forgotten; a censure on the part of the Church authorities also cast a shadow over him. In fact, John Scotus represents a radical Platonism that sometimes seems to approach a pantheistic vision, even though his personal subjective intentions were always orthodox. Some of John Scotus Erigena's works have come down to us among which the following in particular deserve mention: the Treatise *"On the Division of Nature"* and the expositions on *"The Heavenly Hierarchy"* of St Dionysius. In them he continues to develop stimulating theological and spiritual reflections which could suggest an interesting furthering of knowledge also to contemporary theologians. I refer, for example, to what he wrote on the duty of exercising an appropriate discernment on what is presented as *auctoritas vera*, or on the commitment to continue the quest for the truth until one achieves some experience of it in the silent adoration of God.

Our author says: "*Salus nostra ex fide inchoat:* our salvation begins with faith"; in other words we cannot speak of God starting with our own inventions but rather with what God says of himself in the Sacred Scriptures. Since, however, God tells only the truth, Scotus Erigena is convinced that the authority and reason can never contradict each other; he is convinced that true religion and true philosophy coincide. In this perspective he writes: "Any type of authority that is not confirmed by true reason must be considered weak.... Indeed there is no true authority other than that which coincides with the truth, discovered by virtue of reason, even should one be dealing with an authority recommended and handed down for the use of the successors of the holy Fathers" (I, *PL* 122, col. 513 BC). Consequently, he warns: "Let no authority intimidate you or distract you from what makes you understand the conviction obtained through correct rational contemplation. Indeed, the authentic authority never contradicts right reason, nor can the latter ever contradict a true authority. "The one and the other both come indisputably from the same source, which is divine wisdom" (I *PL* 122, col. 511 B). We see here a brave affirmation of the value of reason, founded on the certainty that the true authority is reasonable, because God is creative reason.

According to Erigena, Scripture itself does not escape the need to be approached with the same criterion of discernment. In fact, although Scripture comes from God the Irish theologian maintains, proposing anew a reflection made earlier by John Chrysostom it would not be necessary had the human being not sinned. It must therefore be deduced that Scripture was given by God with a pedagogical intention and with indulgence so that man might remember all that had been impressed within his heart from the moment of his creation, "in the image and likeness of God" (cf. *Gn* 1: 26) and that the Fall of man had caused him to forget. Erigena writes in his *Expositiones:* "It is not man who was created for Scripture, which he would not have needed had he not sinned, but rather it is Scripture, interwoven with doctrine and symbols, which was given to man. Thanks to Scripture, in fact, our rational nature may be introduced to the secrets of authentic and pure contemplation of God" (II, *PL* 122, col. 146 C). The words of Sacred Scripture purify our somewhat blind reason and help us to recover the memory of what we, as the image of God, carry in our hearts, unfortunately wounded by sin.

From this derive certain hermeneutical consequences, concerning the way to interpret Scripture, that still today can point out the right approach for a correct reading of Sacred Scripture. In fact it is a question of discovering the hidden meaning in the sacred text and this implies a special inner exercise through which reason is open to the sure road to the truth. This exercise consists in cultivating constant readiness for conversion. Indeed, to acquire an in-depth vision of the text it is necessary to progress at the same time in conversion of the heart and in the conceptual analysis of the biblical passage, whether it is of a cosmic, historical or doctrinal character. Indeed, it is only by means of a constant purification of both the eye of the heart and the eye of the mind that it is possible to arrive at an exact understanding.

Works of Dionysius the Areopagite, from the verse Prologue of Scotus Erigena addressed to Charles the Bald, Latin 1618, f. 4, Bibliothèque Nationale de France

ONO GLORIOSISSIMO REGI
KAROLO LVDOVICI IMPATORIS FILIO

Carolus
fil. Lud

vmine sydereo dionisius auxit athenas.

A riopagites magnificusq; sophos

P rimo comot' phebo subeunte selena.

T empore q's tauro fixus erat dns.

M ox ut conuersus mira stupefact' elysii.

C onsequit gaudens ierothea ducem .   deest uerssq

P neumatis excelsi fonte renat' erat.

E c mora pfulgens celestis luce sophye.

T rydas edocuit de quib; ort' adest.

A nq; ferunt paulu q xpm sparsit in orbe.

P si felices imposuisse manus.

S t mox pfect' doctous symmachus instar.

A ex cecropidas puigil archyereus.

P ta dehinc uolitans paulu sub astra secut'.

A mpiru celi. tercia regna uidet.

E uscipit at seraphym pmos scos q; cherubym.

S etherios q; tronos q sedet ipse ds .

A ost hos uirtutes domminat' atq; potentes.

P gminib; sacris enitet ordo sequens .

ΑΡΧ ΩΗΑΡΧΑΡΕΛ ΩΝ ΤΕ ΧΟ ΡΩΝ ΑΓΕΛ ΩΝΤΕΤΕ ΛΛΥΓΩΗ

ᴣᴣ enab: oyraniis tcia taxis inest.

Η os q numeros terno ter limite septos

Ρ redicti patris mystica dicta docent.

HAEC INSVNT INSVNT IN HOC DE IERARCHIA CELESTI. TOTV CAPITVLV̈ XV.

m omis diuina illuminatio scdm bonitate uarie inpulsa

puemens manet simpla ᵗꝯ̃ hoc solu s: ꞿ unificat illuminata.

q m pulchre diuina ꞿ celestia etia p dissimilia symbola

manifestant. Q uid ꞷ ierarchia ꞿ que p ierarchia

intelligentia. Q uid significat anglox cognominatio.

uare omis celestes essentie comunit angli dicuntur.

ue pima celestiu essentiaru dispositio. que media que ultima.

e seraphin ꞿ cherubin ꞿ tronis ꞿ de pima eox ierachia.

e domnationib; ꞿ uirtutib: ꞿ potestatib: ꞿ de media eox ierarchia.

e principib; ꞿ archanglis ꞿ anglis ꞿ de ultima eox ierarchia.

This arduous, demanding and exciting journey, that consists of continuous achievements and the relativisation of human knowledge, leads the intelligent creature to the threshold of the divine Mystery where all notions admit of their own weakness and inability and thus, with the simple free and sweet power of the truth, make it obligatory ceaselessly to surpass all that is progressively achieved. Worshipful and silent recognition of the Mystery which flows into unifying communion is therefore revealed as the only path to a relationship with the truth that is at the same time the most intimate possible and the most scrupulously respectful of otherness. John Scotus, here too using terminology dear to the Christian tradition of the Greek language, called this experience for which we strive "theosis", or divinisation, with such daring affirmations that he might be suspected of heterodox pantheism. Yet, even today one cannot but be strongly moved by texts such as the following in which with recourse to the ancient metaphor of the smelting of iron he writes: "just as all red-hot iron is liquified to the point that it seems nothing but fire and yet the substances remain distinct from one another, so it must be accepted that after the end of this world all nature, both the corporeal and the incorporeal, will show forth God alone and yet remain integral so that God can in a certain way be com-prehended while remaining in-comprehensible and that the creature itself may be transformed, with ineffable wonder, and reunited with God" (V, *PL* 122, col. 451 B).

In fact, the entire theological thought of John Scotus is the most evident demonstration of the attempt to express the expressible of the inexpressible God, based solely upon the mystery of the Word made flesh in Jesus of Nazareth. The numerous metaphors John Scotus used to point out this ineffable reality show how aware he was of the absolute inadequacy of the terms in which we speak of these things. And yet the enchantment and that aura of authentic mystical experience, which every now and then one can feel tangibly in his texts, endures. As proof of this it suffices to cite a passage from *De divisione naturae* which touches in depth even our mind as believers of the 21st century: "We should desire nothing", he writes, "other than the joy of the truth that is Christ, avoid nothing other than his absence. The greatest torment of a rational creature consists in the deprivation or absence of Christ. Indeed this must be considered the one cause of total and eternal sorrow. Take Christ from me and I am left with no good thing nor will anything terrify me so much as his absence. The greatest torments of a rational creature are the deprivation and absence of him" (V, *PL* 122, col. 989a). These are words that we can make our own, translating them into a prayer to the One for whom our hearts long.

Saints Cyril and Methodius

I would like to explore Cyril and Methodius, brothers by blood and in the faith, the so-called "Apostles to the Slavs". Cyril was born in Thessalonica to Leo, an imperial magistrate, in 826 or 827. He was the youngest of seven. As a child he learned the Slavonic language. When he was 14 years old he was sent to Constantinople to be educated and was companion to the young Emperor, Michael III. In those years Cyril was introduced to the various university disciplines, including dialectics, and his teacher was Photius. After refusing a brilliant marriage he decided to receive holy Orders and became "librarian" at the Patriarchate. Shortly afterwards, wishing to retire in solitude, he went into hiding at a monastery but was soon discovered and entrusted with teaching the sacred and profane sciences. He carried out this office so well that he earned the nickname of "Philosopher". In the meantime, his brother Michael (born in about 815), left the world after an administrative career in Macedonia, and withdrew to a monastic life on Mount Olympus in Bithynia, where he was given the name "Methodius" (a monk's monastic name had to

Head of Saints Cyril and Methodius, brass, Kreuzenstein Castle, Austria begin with the same letter as his baptismal name) and became hegumen of the Monastery of Polychron.

Attracted by his brother's example, Cyril too decided to give up teaching and go to Mount Olympus to meditate and pray. A few years later (in about 861), the imperial government sent him on a mission to the Khazars on the Sea of Azov who had asked for a scholar to be sent to them who could converse with both Jews and Saracens. Cyril, accompanied by his brother Methodius, stayed for a long time in Crimea where he learned Hebrew and sought the body of Pope Clement I who had been exiled there. Cyril found Pope Clement's tomb and, when he made the return journey with his brother, he took Clement's precious relics with him. Having arrived in Constantinople the two brothers were sent to Moravia by the Emperor Michael III, who had received a specific request from Prince Ratislav of Moravia: "Since our people rejected paganism", Ratislav wrote to Michael, "they have embraced the Christian law; but we do not have a teacher who can explain the true faith to us in our own language". The mission was soon unusually successful. By translating the liturgy into the Slavonic language the two brothers earned immense popularity.

However, this gave rise to hostility among the Frankish clergy who had arrived in Moravia before the Brothers and considered the territory to be under their ecclesiastical jurisdiction. In order to justify themselves, in 867 the two brothers travelled to Rome. On the way they stopped in Venice, where they had a heated discussion with the champions of the so-called "trilingual heresy" who claimed that there were only three languages in which it was lawful to praise God: Hebrew, Greek and Latin. The two brothers obviously forcefully opposed this claim. In Rome Cyril and Methodius were received by Pope Adrian II who led a procession to meet them in order to give a dignified welcome to St Clement's relics. The Pope had also realised the great importance of their exceptional mission. Since the middle of the first millennium, in fact, thousands of Slavs had settled in those territories located between the two parts of the Roman Empire, the East and the West, whose relations were fraught with tension. The Pope perceived that the Slav peoples would be able to serve as a bridge and thereby help to preserve the union between the Christians of both parts of the Empire. Thus he did not hesitate to approve the mission of the two brothers in Great Moravia, accepting and approving the use of the Slavonic language in the liturgy. The Slavonic Books were laid on the altar of St Mary of Phatmé (St Mary Major) and the liturgy in the Slavonic tongue was celebrated in the Basilicas of St Peter, St Andrew and St Paul.

Unfortunately, Cyril fell seriously ill in Rome. Feeling that his death was at hand, he wanted to consecrate himself totally to God as a monk in one of the Greek monasteries of the City (probably Santa Prassede) and took the monastic name of Cyril (his baptismal name was Constantine). He then insistently begged his brother Methodius, who in the meantime had been ordained a Bishop, not to abandon their mission in Moravia and to return to the peoples there. He addressed this prayer to God: "Lord, my God... hear my prayers and keep the flock you have entrusted to me faithful... Free them from the heresy of the three languages, gather them all in unity and make the people you have chosen agree in the true faith and confession". He died on 14 February 869.

Faithful to the pledge he had made with his brother, Methodius returned to Moravia and Pannonia (today, Hungary) the following year, 870, where once again he encountered the violent aversion of the Frankish missionaries who took him prisoner. He did not lose heart and when he was released in 873, he worked hard to organise the Church and train a group of disciples. It was to the merit of these disciples that it was possible to survive the crisis unleashed after the death of Methodius on 6 April 885: persecuted and imprisoned, some of them were sold as slaves and taken to Venice where they were redeemed by a Constantinopolitan official who allowed them to return to the countries of the Slavonic Balkans. Welcomed in Bulgaria, they were able to continue the mission that Methodius had begun and to disseminate the Gospel in the "Land of the Rus". God with his mysterious Providence thus availed himself of their persecution to save the work of the holy Brothers. Literary documentation of their work is extant. It suffices to think of texts such as the *Evangeliarium* (liturgical passages of the New Testament), the *Psalter*, various *liturgical texts* in Slavonic, on which both the Brothers had worked. Indeed, after Cyril's death, it is to Methodius and to his disciples that we owe the translation of the entire *Sacred Scriptures*, the *Nomocanone* and the *Book of the Fathers*.

Wishing now to sum up concisely the profile of the two Brothers, we should first recall the enthusiasm with which Cyril approached the writings of St Gregory of Nazianzus, learning from him the value of language in the transmission of the Revelation. St Gregory had expressed the wish that Christ would speak through him: "I am a servant of the Word, so I put myself at the service of the Word". Desirous of imitating Gregory in this service, Cyril asked Christ to deign to speak in Slavonic through him. He introduced his work of translation with the solemn invocation: "Listen, O all of you

Cyril and Methodius, apostles to the Slavs, stained glass window designed by Alfons Mucha, St Vitus Church, Prague

Slav Peoples, listen to the word that comes from God, the word that nourishes souls, the word that leads to the knowledge of God". In fact, a few years before the Prince of Moravia had asked the Emperor Michael III to send missionaries to his country, it seems that Cyril and his brother Methodius, surrounded by a group of disciples, were already working on the project of collecting the Christian dogmas in books written in Slavonic. The need for new graphic characters closer to the language spoken was therefore clearly apparent: so it was that the Glagolitic alphabet came into being. Subsequently modified, it was later designated by the name "Cyrillic", in honour of the man who inspired it. It was a crucial event for the development of the Slav civilisation in general. Cyril and Methodius were convinced that the individual peoples could not claim to have received the Revelation fully unless they had heard it in their own language and read it in the characters proper to their own alphabet.

Methodius had the merit of ensuring that the work begun by his brother was not suddenly interrupted. While Cyril, the "Philosopher", was more inclined to contemplation, Methodius on the other hand had a leaning for the active life. Thanks to this he was able to lay the foundations of the successive affirmation of what we might call the "Cyrillian-Methodian idea": it accompanied the Slav peoples in the different periods of their history, encouraging their cultural, national and religious development. This was already recognised by Pope Pius XI in his Apostolic Letter *Quod Sanctum Cyrillum*, in which he described the two Brothers: "Sons of the East, with a Byzantine homeland, of Greek origin, for the Roman missions to reap Slav apostolic fruit" (*AAS* 19 [1927] 93-96). The historic role they played was later officially proclaimed by Pope John Paul II who, with his Apostolic Letter

Egregiae Virtutis, declared them Co-Patrons of Europe, together with St Benedict (31 December 1980; *L'Osservatore Romano* English edition, 19 January 1981, p. 3).

Cyril and Methodius are in fact a classic example of what today is meant by the term "inculturation": every people must integrate the message revealed into its own culture and express its saving truth in its own language. This implies a very demanding effort of "translation" because it requires the identification of the appropriate words to present anew, without distortion, the riches of the revealed word. The two holy Brothers have left us a most important testimony of this, to which the Church also looks today in order to draw from it inspiration and guidelines.

Double page spread: *translation of the remains of St Cyril from the Vatican to the church of San Clemente in Rome*, fresco, Basilica of San Clemente

S MI
CHAEL

CLEMENS:

на своа мефодьа и костантина · и слышавь левь · въско
рѣ посла а · и придоста къ цсрю · и прѣмь а присла комнѣ
словеньскаа земла · просащи оучитела собѣ · и могль
бы имь проттолковати стыа книгы · сего бо желаюноу
моленабыстацрм · и поидоша въ словеньскоуземлю ·
к ростиславоу · и стополкоу · и коцелоу · сима прише д шима
нача ста составлати писмена азбоуковнаа · сло
веньскы · и преложи ста аплъ и еуе и ради быша сло
вене · ако слышаша величье бжье · своимь азыкомь ;

По семже преложиша аптлъ · и ахтанкъ · и прочаа кни
гы · нѣцнижи начаша хоулити словеньскаа книгы
глюще · ако не достоить никоторомоуже азыкоу и мѣ
ти въ азъбоуковъ своа · разве евреи · и грькъ · и ла

INDEX OF AUDIENCES

Prince Rotislav of Moravia asking Emperor Michael III to send him missionaries who would preach to the Slavs in their own language, who in turn sends for Cyril and Methodius from Thessalonika, miniature from the *Chronicle of Radziwill*, f. 13, Academy of Sciences, St Petersburg

INDEX OF ILLUSTRATIONS

PICTURE CREDITS